DATE DUE

MAR 02.1999			
DEC.05.2000			
FEB 09 2002			

Crime Detection

CHRIS OXLADE

RIGBY
INTERACTIVE
LIBRARY

Interiors designed by **AMR**
Illustrations by Art Construction
Printed in the United Kingdom

00 99 98 97 96
10 9 8 7 6 5 4 3 2 1

Library of Congress Cataloging-in-Publication Data
Oxlade, Chris.
    Crime detection / Chris Oxlade.
        p.   cm. – (Science encounters)
Includes index.
Summary: Uses familiar examples to explain the science of crimedetection,
covering such aspects as fingerprints, clues in the human body, chemical
evidence, and computers.
        ISBN 1-57572-090-6
        1. Criminal investigation—Juvenile literature
2. Forensic sciences–Juvenile literature.
[Criminal investigation.   2. Forensic sciences.] I. Title. II. Series.
HV8073.8.095   1997
363.3'5–2dc20   96-32567
                                                                   CIP
                                                                   AC

Acknowledgments
The publisher would like to thank the following for permission to reproduce photographs.
Peter Menzel/Science Photo Library, p. 4; Associated Press/Topham, p. 5; James King-
Holmes/Science Photo Library, p. 10; Image Bank, p. 11; Philippe Plailly/Science Photo
Library, p. 12; Michael Gilbert/Science Photo Library, p. 15; Gary S. Chapman/Image Bank,
p. 16; Andrew Syred/Science Photo Library, p. 17; Shout, p. 18; Harvey Pincis/Science Photo
Library, p. 20; Press Association/Topham, p. 21; Alfred Gescheidt/Image Bank, p. 23; Kay
Chernush/Image Bank, p. 24; Will and Deni McIntyre/Science Photo Library, p. 25; Scott
Camazine/Science Photo Library, p. 26; R. Drexel/Bilderberg/Network, p. 27; Topham,.
p. 28, p. 29; Ander McIntyre, p. 7, p. 8, p. 9, p. 22.

Every effort has been made to contact copyright holders of any material reproduced in this book.
Any omissions will be rectified in subsequent printings if notice is given to the publisher.

CONTENTS

SCIENCE IN CRIME FIGHTING

H ow do you think the police use science to
fight and solve crimes? As a matter of fact,
the police use many different kinds of science,
including physics, chemistry, and biology to do their
work. Even solving crimes is a science all by itself. It's
called forensic science. In this book, you can find out
how the police use science to help prevent crime in the
first place and to solve crimes after they have happened.

Crime Prevention

It is much better to prevent a crime than to spend time
and money investigating it afterward, perhaps without
success. Police officers and security people use
science for surveillance (watching and listening)
and to catch criminals as they carry out crimes. For
example, in a shopping center, security cameras watch
all the customers in case one of them tries to steal
from one of the stores. Other examples of where
science helps to prevent crime include burglar
alarms and **X-ray** machines, which search luggage
for suspicious objects.

Evidence collected from
a crime scene is
processed in a forensic
science laboratory.

Forensic Science

Forensic science is the use of science to help solve a crime. Forensic scientists work in laboratories, analyzing evidence that has been collected from the scene of a crime. They try to match the evidence from the scene with evidence from any suspects, or people they think may have committed the crime. These clues are like pieces of a puzzle. For example, tiny specks of paint found under a suspect's fingernails might match the paint from a crime scene.

Forensic scientists show their evidence to courts of law, where criminals are tried for their crimes. These scientists are called expert witnesses, because they are experts on the evidence they present.

Evidence Watch

Every piece of forensic evidence must be looked after carefully, from the time it is found to the time when it is shown in court. A record is kept of every person who handles the evidence. This is to prevent anyone from trying to change it.

Forensic evidence is presented in courts of law during trials. Witnesses are asked questions related to the evidence.

SECURITY SCIENCE

Science does not just help to catch criminals. It also helps to stop crime in the first place. You have probably seen security devices such as video cameras and burglar alarms at your school, in local shops, or even at home. Security devices help to discourage criminals from breaking in somewhere or from stealing. They can also help the police to catch criminals who do carry out the crimes.

Burglar Alarms

A burglar alarm system protects a home, a school, a factory, or other building from being broken into when it is empty, for example, at night or over a weekend. When the system is turned on, it can automatically sense if any doors or windows are opened and if people are walking through the rooms. If the system detects such movement, it sets off an alarm.

The type of infrared sensor used in burglar alarms in homes. The sensor can "see" a much wider area than a human eye.

Magnetic devices called sensors can detect if doors or windows are opened. When the door is closed, an electric switch operated by a magnet in the door frame keeps it closed. When the door opens, the switch is activated. This is detected by the alarm's control panel. An infrared sensor can detect movements. All warm things, such as the human body, give off energy known as infrared radiation. An infrared sensor looks for any infrared radiation coming from a room. If the source of the radiation moves, the sensor sends a signal to the control panel, and the alarm is set off.

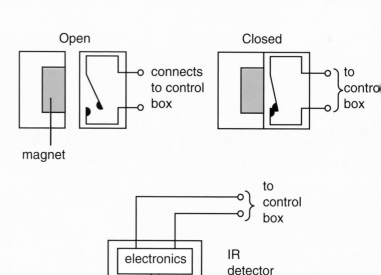

Electronic Locks

Electronic locks stop people from entering a room or building that they aren't allowed to enter. They are much more difficult to break open than simple locks with keys. To open an electronic lock, you have to punch in the correct numbers in the right order on a keypad. Some locks work with a key that looks like a credit card, which you "swipe" past the lock to open it. Other lock systems can examine fingerprints or voice prints, and will allow in only those that they recognize. A voice print is a record of the mixture of sounds in a person's voice. No two voice prints are the same.

This security camera keeps a watchful eye over a busy city street. Many kinds of criminal activity can be recorded and the criminals identified.

Closed-circuit Television

Closed-circuit television cameras keep watch over shops, banks, and busy streets. Sometimes the pictures from the cameras are watched on screens by security guards. In other systems, the pictures are recorded onto videotape. Later, the tape is played back so that any criminal suspects can be identified if a crime has taken place.

ELECTRONIC TAGS

Many clothing stores have electronic tagging machines to stop customers from stealing clothes. Each item in the store has a tag attached to it. If somebody takes something out of the store without paying for it, a sensor at the door detects the electronic tag and sets off an alarm.

FRAUD AND FORGERY

I f you cheat somebody out of money, for example, by using his or her credit card, then you commit a crime called **fraud. Forgery** is a crime that involves making something, such as a bank note, that appears to be real but is not. How does science help to prevent these crimes?

Security Codes

Security codes are used to stop just anyone from using another person's bank accounts or from looking at computer records without permission. Most security codes consist of a list of numbers or letters. For example, to get money from a bank cash machine, you need to type in your own personal identification number (PIN). To look at some computer records you have to enter a password first.

In the future you will not need to give an automatic teller machine (cash machine) a security code. It may be able to recognize your face.

This forged signature has taken a lot of practice. Look how similar the signatures are.

Bank Notes and Cards

The most common way of preventing fraud in stores and banks is to ask a person to sign his or name. This is then compared to the signature already on the person's bank card or credit card. Sometimes, the signature on the card is printed in invisible ink. It only shows up when the ink is lit up by **ultraviolet light** from a special lamp. If criminals cannot see the signature, they cannot copy it.

There are many ways to make forgery more difficult for criminals. Bank notes are printed with many different colors of ink, and the lines that make up the pictures are very thin. This makes the notes difficult to print without the use of very expensive machinery. Some bank notes have a thin metal strip made of a mixture of different metals. The metals in the strip can be tested to find out if the note is real. Bank cards often have **holograms** on them. You need very complicated equipment to make a hologram, so these cards are difficult to copy.

MOBILE PHONES

When you use a mobile telephone, it sends a security code to the telephone company. The company needs the correct code before it lets the user make a call. Unfortunately, criminals can detect the radio signals from some mobile phones and copy the signals into stolen phones. All the charges from the stolen phone are then sent to the person using the real phone.

CRIME ON THE MOVE

Science helps to catch people who break the law as they travel. With the help of X rays and magnets, security machines can find hidden things, such as illegal guns, in luggage or clothing. Radar devices can trap and record motorists who break the speed limit. It is even possible to keep track of exactly where a stolen car is located.

Airport Security

Airport security officers try to prevent people from carrying guns or explosives onto aircraft, where they could be used in a hijack. During a security check all luggage must pass through an X-ray scanner before it can go onto the aircraft. X rays pass right through most materials, but dense materials like metals don't let them through. When X rays are sent through a bag with a gun inside it, the outline of the gun shows up.

Passengers cannot go through an airport X-ray machine, because exposure to too many X rays can harm the body. Instead, they walk through a metal detector, which detects any large pieces of metal they might be carrying in their pockets, such as a gun. A metal detector works by setting up a **magnetic field** around an object. Any metal that enters the magnetic field changes the field's shape. This change is detected by the machine's electronics, and an alarm is set off.

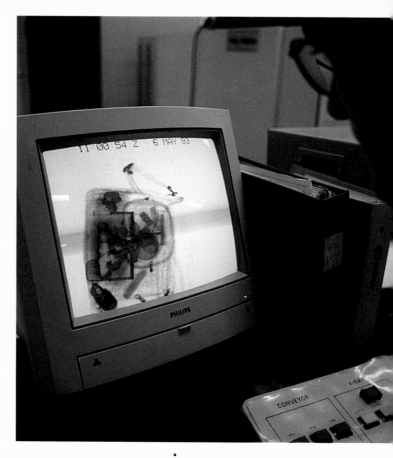

An X-ray scanner operator looks for signs of suspicious objects in a purse.

A speed camera looks for cars that travel faster than the speed limit on a city road. It measures the cars' speeds as they approach.

FOLLOW THAT CAR!

There are devices that can be hidden inside a car to show police where the car is located if it is ever reported stolen. Police send out a radio signal, which turns on the device in the car. The devise sends out its own signal. The police then follow the signal to find the stolen car.

Radar Guns

A speed gun figures out the speed of a moving vehicle. It works by radar, which is short for *r*adio *d*etection *a*nd *r*anging. Radar sends out radio waves and detects any that bounce back. The time it takes for the waves to travel back tells the machine how far away a vehicle is. By taking two readings a split second apart, the machine can figure out the vehicle's speed. Roadside speed cameras have a built-in radar gun. They automatically take a photograph of any cars that go over the speed limit. The owner can be traced from the car's license plate.

CRIME SCENE CLUES

The police know that even the smartest criminals leave behind signs that they were at the scene of a crime. These signs are called evidence. The police use evidence to try to find criminals. As soon as the police arrive at the scene of a crime, they make sure that nothing is moved. Then the scene is photographed, and the exact position of all the evidence is measured and recorded. Finally, the evidence is collected. Some pieces of evidence are so small that they can be seen only with a **microscope.**

Hidden Prints

Fingerprints are some of the most important clues that forensic scientists can find. Fingerprints are normally invisible, but they show up when you dust them with fine powder. Then they can be moved to sticky tape and photographed. At the crime scene, all the possible places where the criminal could have left fingerprints are dusted.

Brushing surfaces with fine magnetic powder makes any fingerprints show up.

Other Evidence

Police wear gloves to collect evidence so that they do not put their own fingerprints on it. Small items of evidence, such as pieces of glass, hairs, fibers from fabrics, and pieces of soil, are sucked into a vacuum cleaner and trapped in a **filter.** Small samples of blood stains are collected on **swabs.** Every piece of evidence is put into a separate plastic bag and carefully labeled so it does not get mixed up with other items.

A Murder Scene

At the scene of a murder, the position of the dead person's body is photographed, measured, and marked. Then the body is taken away for scientists to try to figure out when and how the person died. Sometimes a body is found years after the person has died, and only the skeleton is left. In this case, scientists have to figure out who the person was, as well as the cause of death.

PLASTER PRINTS

Fingerprints are not the only prints that forensic scientists look for. They also collect footprints and tire tracks. A copy of the print or track is made by pouring **plaster** into it and letting the plaster set. The scientists then try to match the prints to shoes or vehicles of possible suspects.

The outline on the ground shows where a body was found.

FINGERPRINTS

There are billions of people in the world, but do you know what makes you different from all other people? The answer is your fingerprints. They are unique. Nobody else in the world has fingerprints with the same pattern of lines as yours. Every time you touch something, you leave your fingerprints on it (unless you are wearing gloves). Fingerprints are the best way of identifying people. The police can use them to find out who has been at the scene of a crime.

A Person's Mark

Fingerprints are caused by the ridges and grooves on your fingertips. If your fingers have dirt or paint on them and you touch something, they leave prints that can easily be seen and photographed. Even if your fingers are clean, they still leave traces of sweat and natural oils that are always on your skin. These fingerprints can be found by brushing them with fine powder, which sticks to the sweat and oil. Fingerprints on paper and cloth are made to show up with special chemicals (see page 18). Some fingerprints can only be seen by shining **laser** light on them.

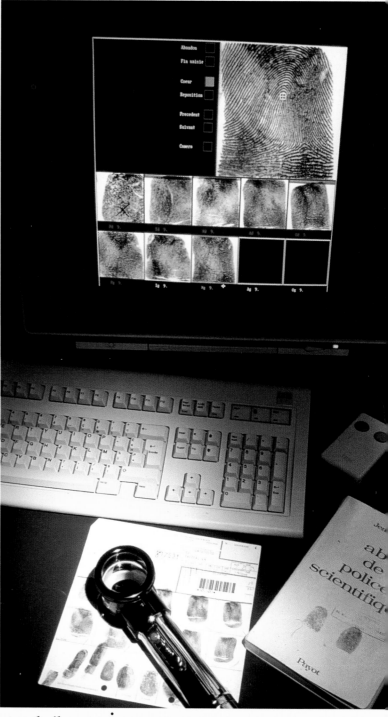

Fingerprint records can be studied on paper and computer.

Fingerprint Records

The police make fingerprint records of all the people known to have been at the scene of a crime. Even people who have nothing to do with the crime have a record made. Any fingerprints found at the scene that match these people's fingerprints can then be put aside. This may leave unknown fingerprints, which could belong to the criminal. The fingerprints of people who have criminal records (have been convicted of crimes) are stored in computer **databases.**

Loops, Whorls, and Arches?

Fingerprint experts group fingerprints according to their patterns. Common shapes in fingerprints are loops, whorls, and arches. By putting together fingerprints in this way the police can match fingerprints found at the scene of a crime with ones that they have in their databases.

MILLIONS OF PRINTS

In the 1880s, a British scientist, Sir Francis Galton (1822–1911), realized that no two people have the same fingerprints. Soon, fingerprinting became a police method for solving crimes. The FBI (Federal Bureau of Investigations), which investigates crimes, has about 80 million fingerprint records. It can take a long time to go through them all to find a match!

Although people have similar fingerprint patterns, no two people have exactly the same ones.

OTHER BODY CLUES

Besides fingerprinting, there are other ways of matching a person to evidence left behind at the scene of a crime. Specks of blood and hairs are especially useful. The blood is tested, and skin and hair are analyzed and then compared to samples taken from suspects.

Blood Groups

Scientists divide human blood into different types, called blood groups. A blood test shows which group a sample of blood belongs to. When a suspect's blood type matches that of blood found at a crime scene, it cannot prove anything. Millions of other people have the same blood group. However, if no match is found, the police may be able to eliminate certain people from their list of suspects.

DNA

DNA stands for **d**eoxyribo**n**ucleic **a**cid. It is a chemical that is found in almost every **cell** in every living thing. DNA is like a recipe for making a person. Everybody's DNA recipe is slightly different, except for identical twins! The pattern of DNA determines the color of hair and eyes and almost everything else about a person's body. DNA is passed from parents to children, which is why you may look like your father or mother.

DNA is very complicated. No two people have the same DNA—except identical twins.

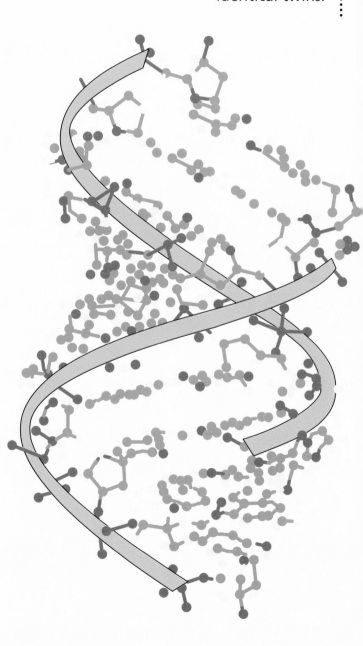

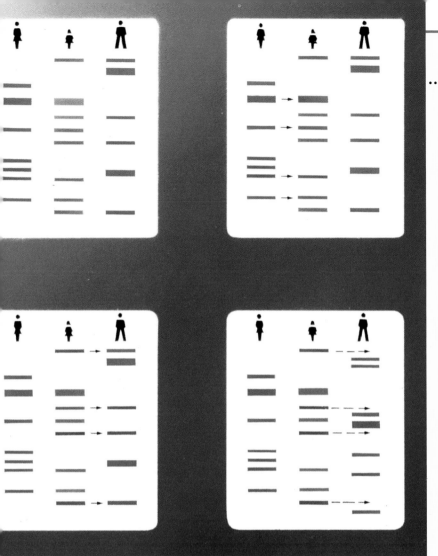

Each picture shows three DNA samples (from a woman, a child, and a man). The first three show that the child received some DNA from each of his or her parents. The last picture shows that the man cannot be the child's father.

DNA Profiling

A DNA profile is made using blood and other body substances collected from a crime scene. The process of making a DNA profile is complicated and takes special laboratory equipment. A profile can only be made from cells, and they must be fresh. Because hair itself is dead, a hair with a root is needed for a DNA profile. Not all blood cells contain DNA, so only certain cells can be used. A finished profile looks like a long strip of film with light and dark bands across it. If the patterns of light and dark on two profiles match, then there is a very good chance that the two samples of DNA came from the same person.

FINGERPRINTS ARE BEST!

Although no two people have the same DNA (except for identical twins), it is possible for the DNA profiles of two people to look the same. So although DNA profiling is a very useful test, it is not as reliable as a good fingerprint!

MICROSCOPIC EVIDENCE

Criminals do not always leave fingerprints at the scene of a crime. So forensic scientists also look for other evidence that could help them to find the criminal. Sometimes they study pieces of evidence from the scene, and try to match them with something belonging to a suspect. For example, a tiny fiber of cloth could be matched to clothes found at a suspect's house. Or a bullet could be matched to a gun found with a suspect's fingerprints on it. To make these matches, scientists have to examine the evidence under a microscope in the forensic laboratory.

Forensic Ballistics

Ballistics is the science of how bullets (and bombs and missiles) are fired and how they travel through the air. The study of forensic ballistics helps the police to match a bullet with the gun from which it was fired. When a bullet is fired, it gets bumped and scratched by the gun. Every gun leaves its own set of marks on a bullet, like a fingerprint. In the laboratory, bullets are studied under a special microscope.

In a similar way, the marks and wounds made by other weapons, such as knives and even human teeth, can also be studied under a microscope. They can be matched to the weapon that made them, or to the teeth that took the bite!

These unused bullets are unmarked. As soon as they are fired, they could be traced to the gun that fired them.

A Closer Look

The tiny pieces of evidence that are found at the scene of a crime are often mixed together. In the laboratory, hairs, fibers, bits of paint, wood, and glass are separated and examined using a **binocular microscope**. This is really two microscopes—one for each eye—that are placed side by side. It allows a scientist to see an object magnified and to see all of its sides.

Most substances that are not from living things are made up of crystals. Forensic scientists use a **polarizing microscope** to help identify crystals, such as drugs. The polarizing microscope makes different crystals show up in different colors.

A photomicrograph (photograph from a microscope) of two different types of fiber. The fibers may have looked the same to the naked eye.

FORGED PAPERS

Like fingers and bullets, typewriters leave their own "fingerprints" on paper. This may happen when a letter is slightly worn down. Many criminals have been caught because the police have been able to match forged paperwork to the typewriter on which it was typed.

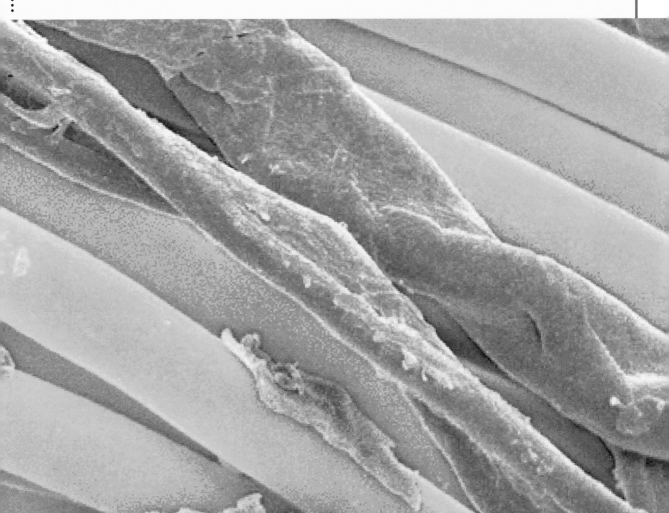

CHEMICAL EVIDENCE

Vital evidence is often present at a crime scene, but it is invisible to the naked eye. So how do forensic scientists find it? The answer is by carrying out chemical tests. Some tests make hidden clues show up. Other tests show which chemicals are in a piece of evidence. Chemical tests may destroy the actual evidence, so forensic scientists only use a small sample of a piece of evidence for their tests.

Chromatograph Tests

Gas **chromatography** is a process that uncovers the chemicals in a sample of evidence and how much of each chemical the sample contains. It is used to test whether things that look the same are really made of the same things. For example, a forged credit card may look like a real one, but it might be made of a slightly different kind of plastic. A test in a gas chromatograph machine can show the difference. A breath-test machine is a special kind of chromatograph that detects the amount of alcohol present on a person's breath. It is used to find out how much alcohol a driver has drunk.

This driver has been stopped by the police and asked to take a breath test. If the test shows that the driver has drunk more alcohol than is permitted by law before driving, there will be a severe penalty.

Fingerprints Uncovered

Fingerprints on rough surfaces, such as paper and cloth, cannot be seen by simply dusting them with powder (see page 12). Instead, the surface has to be soaked in a chemical called ninhydrin. This reacts with the chemicals in the sweat on the fingerprint. It makes new chemicals, which show up as a dark color and make the fingerprint pattern appear.

Comparison Test

Spectrophotometry is another way of testing if two substances are the same. A spectrophotometer is an instrument that detects light rays that are invisible to human eyes. For example, a spectrophotometer might be able to spot the difference between two types of black paint.

Ninhydrin testing reveals fingerprints that might not appear during tests with powder.

TEST RESULTS

The results from a gas chromatograph test can be compared with information about thousands of different products. The information is supplied by the companies that make the product. For example, when the police find a forged credit card, a gas chromatograph test may help them figure out in which factory the card's plastic was made. The factory can then give the police a list of all the people who bought that particular plastic.

MEDICAL EVIDENCE

Forensic medicine is the branch of medicine that investigates suspicious deaths. It helps the police to figure out how the person died and exactly when the death took place. Even if the cause of a person's death seems very clear, forensic scientists look carefully at the body. There may be other, hidden injuries that are not so clear at first. The body of a dead person is taken from the scene of a crime to a **pathology** laboratory for examination.

Tools of the Trade

In the pathology laboratory, a forensic pathologist studies the body to find out how the person died. This process is called an autopsy, or post-mortem examination. The pathologist makes notes of any marks and wounds on the outside of the body and takes photographs of them. Then the body's internal (inside) **organs** are examined. Other specialists may be called in to help, such as a forensic toxicologist, who looks for evidence of poisons or drugs in the body. Any pieces of bullet or knife found in the body are removed and used to help the police find the murder weapon— and the murderer.

A forensic pathologist studies samples of body tissues in a pathology laboratory.

These murder weapons, seized soon after a terrorist attack, will be examined for clues that link them to the attack and the victims' injuries.

Time of Death

It is important to figure out when a person died. If a suspect was seen somewhere other than the scene of the murder at the time of death, then that person cannot be the murderer. After a person dies, the body temperature begins to fall. A few hours later, muscles begin to stiffen. These are clues to the time of death. If a person has been dead for a few days before being discovered, the body begins to rot, or decompose. A pathologist can guess how long the person has been dead by the amount of **decomposition** in the body.

INSECT CLUES

Forensic entomologists (scientists who study insects) study maggots, which are tiny insects that feed on dead bodies. The age of the maggots gives a good clue to how long a person has been dead. The kind of maggot can even show scientists in which area of the country the person died.

BODY OF EVIDENCE

It may take months—even years—before a dead person's body is discovered. Only the skeleton may be left. So how do the police figure out who the person was and how they died? They call in forensic scientists who specialize in finding clues from dead bodies. The scientists study the body's skeleton and teeth and try to build a file of information about the person.

Dental Records

The best clue to a person's identity is the teeth. The size of the teeth and how much they have decayed (rotted), can reveal the person's sex and age. Any dental work on the teeth, such as fillings or false teeth, can also be matched with the dental records of missing people. The use of teeth in this way is called forensic odontology.

Forensic scientists can identify bodies that have been dead for so long that only a skeleton remains. Examining the teeth, or building a face shape (below) can reveal a person's age, sex, name,and sometimes the cause of death.

Skeleton Clues

A skeleton can provide an amazing amount of information about a person. Examinations of skeletons are carried out by forensic anthropologists, who have special knowledge of skeletons and how they grow. The scientist can figure out the person's sex and race from the shape of the skull and pelvis. And the person's age can be estimated by looking at those areas of the bones where growth takes place.

Even if only a few bones of a skeleton are found, the person's height can be estimated. The length and width of the bones are carefully measured and used to calculate the height. The femur (the upper leg bone) is the most useful bone, because it is the longest in the body.

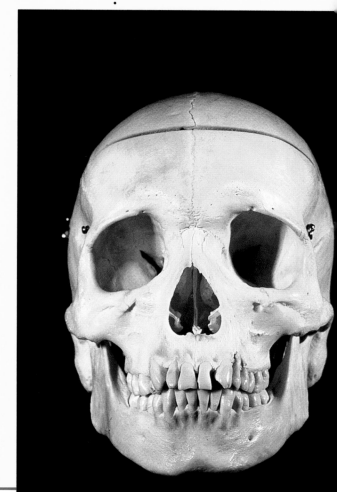

Model Skulls

Forensic anthropologists can use a skull to get an idea of what the dead person's face looked like. A model skull is made from the dead person's skull, and then clay is used to build the areas of skin on the model. The thickness of skin changes over different parts of the face, and the model maker uses this knowledge to build a likeness of the dead person. Pictures of the finished model are shown to the public to find out if anyone recognizes the face.

BONE FACTS

It is not always easy or accurate to estimate a person's age from individual bones. On average, men are taller than women. And various factors, such as diet and environment, can affect a person's height. Also, people begin to shrink by about .02 inches a year after the age of 30!

This face, shown over a skull, shows how the shape of the face depends on the skull.

CRIME FIGHTING TESTS

After the police have arrested a suspect, they can use certain tests to find out whether the suspect is telling the truth or lying. They can use another test to find out if the suspect is mentally ill. A different type of test can be used to find handwriting clues on what look like blank sheets of paper. These tests are carried out by specially trained scientists.

Lie Detectors

A lie detector test does exactly what you might think—it tries to show whether a suspect is telling the truth. A lie detector machine (sometimes called a polygraph) measures a person's **pulse rate, blood pressure,** breathing rate, and how much they sweat. It then prints the results on paper. At the same time the machine makes these measurements, the person is asked questions. If the person lies, the pulse rate, breathing rate, and so on are likely to change. Any changes will show up on the machine. In some countries evidence from lie detectors can be used in court. In many other countries, however, the lawmakers do not believe that the tests are reliable enough to use.

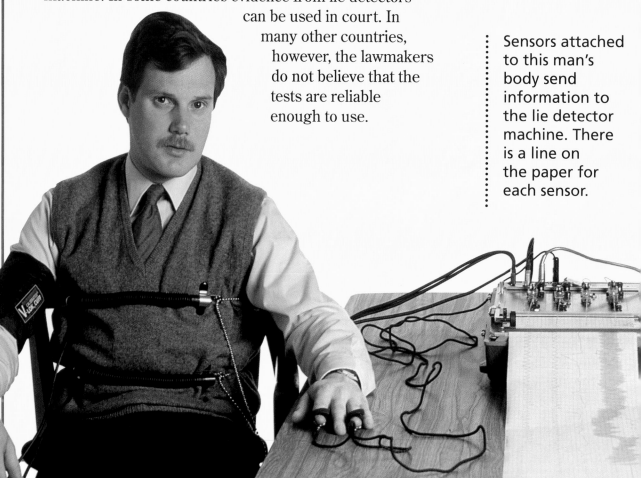

Sensors attached to this man's body send information to the lie detector machine. There is a line on the paper for each sensor.

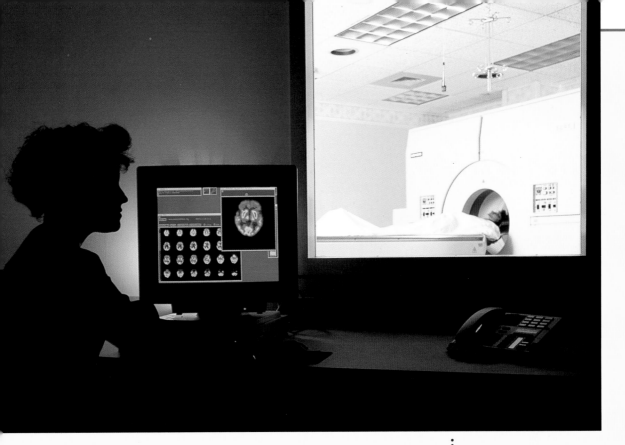

Brain Scans

In some cases, murderers plead mental illness as a defense, saying that they did commit a crime but that they did not know that they were doing something wrong. In a few cases, the murderer is given a brain scan to check the brain. This is done by a machine called a PET scanner. It produces pictures of the brain. A **neurologist** may be able to spot any brain problems from the scan. If a problem is noticed, then it is possible that the suspect may have committed the crime without really understanding that it was wrong.

ESDA Test

Imagine that a person has written a forged letter on a pad of notepaper, and sent the letter in the mail. If there are no fingerprints on the paper, how can the police find out where it came from? An ESDA (electrostatic detection apparatus) test might help. It can show what was written on the sheets of paper that have already been torn off the pad. It does this by showing the tiny dents in the pad that were made by a pen moving across the sheets of paper. The dents show up in black, like the writing on a photocopy.

COMPUTERS IN CRIME FIGHTING

Police around the world use computers more and more in their work. Computers are very good at storing huge amounts of information in databases and searching through that information to match, for example, a fingerprint or some other evidence. Police computers hold information about criminals (their real names, any other names they use, photographs, any previous convictions for crimes, and so on), fingerprint records, and information about cases they have investigated in the past. Computers search through these databases to find matches with evidence.

Fingerprint Databases

Most police departments keep fingerprint records on computer. Fingerprints of convicted criminals are entered into the computer with a machine called a scanner. The computer will have a "picture" of every fingerprint that has been scanned. Information about the fingerprints' shapes and sizes is also added. The computer operator uses this information to try to help the police find a match with any unidentified fingerprints found at a crime scene. Any close matches can be shown on the computer screen next to the unidentified print. The computer can search for a fingerprint in seconds. It would take a person hours and hours to do the same search.

This fingerprint has been scanned onto a computer. If fingerprints are found at a crime scene, they too are scanned. The computer can check very quickly through its databases to see if there is a match.

Composites

A composite is a picture of someone's face that is made from a witness's description. A witness is a person who saw a crime take place. The composite may be a picture of a suspect, a murder victim, or even a missing person. Composites are made using computers. The witness sits with the computer artist, picking out different shapes and colors of nose, mouth, eyes, and so on from a series of pictures. They gradually draw a face. The artist can adjust the face in any way with pens and paintbrushes inside the computer. The composite is printed and used on crime posters.

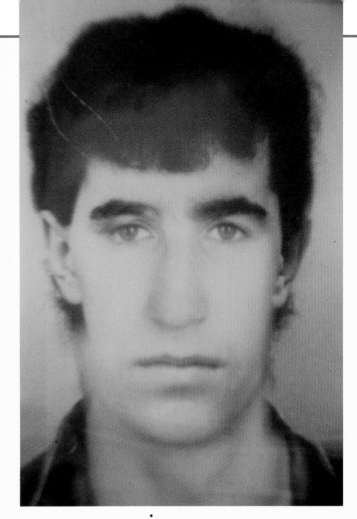

Image Enhancement

In addition to helping to draw pictures of faces, computers can be used to make photographs more clear. This is called image enhancement. A blurred or fuzzy picture is first scanned into the computer. The computer operator then tries to figure out what the original picture looked like. Image enhancement can make a suspect's face clear enough to recognize, or a car's license plate readable.

This composite will be put on public display to help jog the memory of people who may have seen a criminal in action. These people might be able to help catch the criminal.

WHOSE FACE?

In the future, computers may be able to spot faces in photographs or clips of film from a video camera. They could then automatically match the face with photographs in a database of people with criminal records.

GLOSSARY

binocular microscope a microscope with two lenses—one for each eye—that are placed side by side. It allows you to see objects magnified and in three dimensions.

blood pressure measures how well your heart pumps blood around your body

cell the basic building block of all animals and plants. There are hundreds of different types of cells. Each type does its own special job.

chromatography a method that separates the different substances in a mixture

database a store of information held on a computer. The information is arranged so that it is easy for the computer to search through it.

decomposition the process by which the remains of animals and plants break down into other chemicals. It is caused by tiny living things, such as bacteria.

filter a screen with tiny holes in it. It keeps pieces of materials bigger than a certain size from passing through it.

forgery any object (for example a document, a ticket, a bank note, or a painting) that looks like the real thing but is only a copy

fraud a crime in which people make money by lying or using fake documents, for example using a forged credit card

hologram a special kind of photograph that produces a three-dimensional picture when it is lit up

laser a very strong, narrow beam of light. Very powerful lasers can cut through metal.

magnetic field the space around a magnet where the magnet's pull can be felt

microscope an instrument that makes tiny things look much bigger. You look at the things through an eyepiece. There are several different types of microscopes.

neurologist a doctor who specializes in studying the brain and nervous system

organ a part of the body that does a particular job, such as the stomach, the heart, or the lungs

pathology the study of diseases and their effects on the human body

plaster a mixture of powder and water that can be molded into shape and then left to set solid

polarizing microscope a microscope that makes tiny crystals of different substances show up in different colors

pulse rate the number of times a person's heart beats every minute

spectrophotometry a method of figuring out which chemicals are in a substance. This is done by measuring how the substance gives off different colors of light.

swab a piece of material that soaks up liquid. Swabs are used to collect liquid evidence, such as blood.

ultraviolet light a type of light that human eyes cannot detect. When it hits some substances, it makes them give off light that can be seen.

X ray ray of light that can pass through less dense substances, such as skin. X rays are stopped by more dense substances, such as metals.

FACT FILE

- The famous artist Leonardo da Vinci often smoothed paint with his fingers. His fingerprints show up on some of his paintings and are sometimes used to identify fake paintings.

- Most burglar alarms have a four-digit security code. The number is entered on a keypad that has the digits 0 to 9. When a burglar tries to guess the code, they have a 10,000 to 1 chance of getting it right.

- A night terror is a dream during which a person becomes violent and may kill somebody, without even knowing it. Suspects sometimes claim that they committed their crime because they suffer from night terrors. Their brain activity is measured during sleep to see if it is abnormal.

- Forensic ballistics can show the place from which a bullet was fired, as well as which gun fired it.

- DNA profiling is used to link people to other people as well as people to evidence. It can prove, for example, that two people are related to each other.

- Martin Tytell, who lives and works in New York, is known as Mr. Typewriter. If you give him a sheet of paper with typing on it, he can probably name the exact model of typewriter that produced it.

- Satellites in space can see and photograph some types of illegal activity on the earth's surface. One example is their use to spot fields of illegal drugs being grown in hard-to-find areas of mountains or jungles.

FURTHER READINGS

Heckman, Philip. *The Magic of Holography.* Franklin Watts, 1986.

Graham, Ian. *Fakes and Forgeries.* Raintree Steck-Vaughn, 1995.

Italia, Bob. *Courageous Crimefighters.* Oliver Press, 1995.

Markle, Sandra. *Science to the Rescue.* Atheneum, 1994.

INDEX